CD Included

BERKLEE PRESS

Bluegrass Fiddle
and Beyond

Etudes and Ideas
for the Modern Fiddler

by Matt Glaser

Edited by Jonathan Feist

Berklee Press

Vice President: David Kusek
Dean of Continuing Education: Debbie Cavalier
Chief Operating Officer: Robert F. Green
Managing Editor: Jonathan Feist
Editorial Assistants: Yousun Choi, Emily Goldstein, Martin Fowler
Assistant to Matt Glaser: Susan Buzzard

Cover Design: Eric Gould
Cover/Author Photo: Nancy Adler

All music is copyright Matt's Music, 2009, with the exception of "The Girl I Left Behind Me" and "That Tumble-Down Shack in Athlone."

ISBN 978-0-87639-108-2

1140 Boylston Street
Boston, MA 02215-3693 USA
(617) 747-2146
Visit Berklee Press Online at
www.berkleepress.com

DISTRIBUTED BY

HAL•LEONARD®
CORPORATION
7777 W. BLUEMOUND RD. P.O. BOX 13819
MILWAUKEE, WISCONSIN 53213
Visit Hal Leonard Online at
www.halleonard.com

CONTENTS

CD TRACKS

Musicians

Matt Glaser, Violin

John McGann, Mandolin and Guitar

Jim Whitney, Bass

Jimmy Ryan, Mandolin (Tracks 1 and 2)

Tony Trischka, Banjo (Tracks 1 and 2)

Recorded at Arbor Vitae Studios (John McGann, Engineer)

PREFACE

Welcome to a book of etudes, exercises, and ideas that will help you develop your technical and improvisational skills in the world of contemporary fiddling. This world has exploded in the last twenty years, thanks largely to the effort of Mark O'Connor, who has demonstrated that it's possible to play various forms of fiddle music, jazz, and contemporary classical music, all at a very high technical level, and sometimes even simultaneously! I have been part of this world for a long time, teaching at both Mark's and Jay Ungar's camps since their inception. For twenty-eight years, I have observed (and participated in) the scene from my post as chair of the string department at Berklee College of Music.

Over the last few years, I have tried to focus my teaching to help fiddlers develop compositional and intellectual skills applied to their instrument, in real time. Put another way, fiddle players should not be automatons, letting their fingers run rampant. Instead, they should have a comprehensive mental map of music in their heads, as well as a wide range of musical skills that would make them employable in a band setting. The exercises and etudes in this book are designed to help you grow technically on your instrument, while at the same time develop a comprehensive understanding of the inner workings of music.

Some of the etudes in this book are designed to help you grow melodically, others harmonically, and others rhythmically. Melody, harmony, and rhythm are the three elements of music, and as a contemporary improviser, you will need to find methods that help you grow in each of these areas.

SOME WORDS ABOUT BOWING

Bluegrass fiddling is improvisational in nature, and its bowing must be, likewise, improvisational. What this means in practice is that you should master a small number of bowing patterns and be able to mix and match these patterns as well as intersperse them with separate bow strokes. You will notice that most of the etudes in this book do not have specific bowing patterns indicated. I would like you to experiment with different combinations of two-note slurs, three-note slurs, and separate bow strokes. (In the example below you will see four common bowing patterns). Your bowing should always follow and be in the service of the shape of the line and its articulation and dynamics.

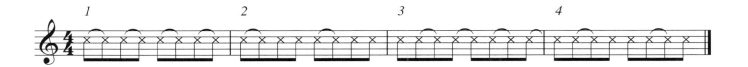

PLAYING ALONG WITH THE CD

The CD accompanying this book includes performances of all the etudes featuring the violin with full band and those same tracks without the violin. I would urge you to spend a lot of time playing along with the violin track. This will help you imitate the bowing, articulation, and dynamics discussed above. Only after you've gotten a really strong sense of the way I play these etudes should you begin to play them along with the rhythm tracks. The worst use of your time would be merely to read the sheet music and play along with the rhythm tracks, because this would neither develop your ear nor allow you to imitate details of sound and articulation that the violin track demonstrates. Before even picking up your violin, you should listen to the tracks a number of times while visually following along with the music. As the great jazz pedagogue John LaPorta said, "You should learn to see what music sounds like and hear what music looks like."

TRACK 1   TRACK 2

The first two tracks on the CD feature two of the songs we study later, presented as they would be in an extended performance. The other tracks are designed to focus more on the violin part so that you can isolate the techniques I present.

You may notice that there are times when what I play on the fiddle differs slightly from what's in the music notation. I did this intentionally so that you could get used to seeing the shape of a line, and then hearing a variation that maintains that shape, but differs slightly in details. This really is the primary message of the book: that you should be able to find the core of a melody and make up variations on that core melody, while retaining its shape.

Let's get started.

CHAPTER 1

Lamb Chops (Skeletal Melody and the Five Levels of Improvisation)

Learning to improvise on a melody is the core message of this book. There are many methods that teach you to improvise on the chords, or underlying harmony of a tune, and that is certainly an important approach. But central to any kind of folk or country improvisation is the ability to identify the essential elements in a melody and improvise on them.

THE FIVE LEVELS OF IMPROVISATION

For many years, I have been teaching a system that I call "The Five Levels of Improvisation." This was originally inspired by the great alto saxophonist Lee Konitz, who teaches a gradual development of a melody that he calls "The Ten Levels of Improvisation." I have taken this approach, modified, and developed it, and organized it so that it may be of value to folks playing music other than jazz.

Before you do anything else, you should try to identify the song's *skeletal melody*. As our musical example, we're going to start with the familiar children's tune "Mary Had a Little Lamb" (don't laugh). You may not think very highly of this melody, but you'd be wrong! Tunes like this have gotten rid of every extraneous element, and have been subjected to what scientists call "Occam's Razor." This principle stipulates that one should not needlessly multiply explanations when fewer would suffice. Simpler is usually better. Tunes such as "Mary Had a Little Lamb" are nicely boiled down to a very simple but valuable progression of pitches. Even so, your first step in improvising on this simple melody is to boil it down even further and try to find a simple skeleton of pitches.

TRACK 3

"Lamb Chops" Full Band

TRACK 4

"Lamb Chops" Play Along

The following examples are presented on track 3 of the CD. Track 4 mutes the fiddle part so that you can practice playing along.

Level 1. Connect with Quarter Notes

Level 1 of our five levels of improvisation is to connect these skeletal tones with constantly moving quarter notes.

Skeleton Embedded in Quarter Notes

Igor Stravinsky wrote in *Poetics of Music*:

My freedom thus consists in my moving about within the narrow frame that I have assigned myself for each one of my undertakings. I shall go even further: my freedom will be so much the greater and more meaningful the more narrowly I limit my field of action   and the more I surround myself with obstacles. Whatever diminishes constraint, diminishes strength. The more constraints one   imposes, the more one frees one's self of the chains that shackle   the spirit.

In this case of the skeletal melody concept, restricting and limiting the field of action paradoxically gives us the freedom to make one small creative gesture.

In "Lamb Chops," I'd like you to play constantly moving quarter notes on the skeletal melody, but only in steps; that is, restrict the way you connect the pitches to stepwise motion—no leaps. That will be level 1A. Level 1B will be for you to connect the skeletal melody in constantly moving quarter notes in leaps—no steps. Finally, level 1C will be for you to connect the skeletal melody in constantly moving quarter notes with some chromaticism added.

Level 2. Constantly Moving Eighth Notes

Keeping the same skeletal melody, you're now going to apply constantly moving eighth notes. Level 2 A, B, and C are as above. In each case, connect the skeletal melody with constantly moving eighth notes (a) in steps, (b) in leaps, and (c) with chromaticism.

Skeleton Embedded in Eighth Notes

Level 3. Rhythmic Variations

In level 3, I'm going to ask you to shift your focus slightly, and make up rhythmic variations on the skeletal melody.

In the first two levels, you were restricted rhythmically to playing constantly moving quarters or eighths. Here you're free to play any rhythms you want as long as you play the skeletal melody.

Jazz Rhythm over Skeleton

Level 4. Counterpoint

Level 4 asks you to play counterpoint to a melody. This is an extremely important but rarely discussed component of great improvisers in any idiom. The best way to begin thinking about this level is to imagine a band with a singer, where some instrumentalist is playing tasty backup while the singer sings. That tasty backup is essentially counterpoint to a melody. Your counterpoint should be relatively still while the melody is moving, and relatively active while the melody is still. You should get to the point where you can keep a melody going in your head while playing counterpoint on your instrument. This bifurcated hearing is something that exists in all styles of music other than western classical. To practice this, I recommend you tape yourself playing a melody, and then play that recording back at a medium volume while improvising a counterpoint. Over time, you should gradually turn the volume down on your recording until you can keep it going entirely in your head without reference to an external audio source.

A lot of great jazz solos are constructed using this principle. For instance, the Charlie Parker line "Ornithology" is written on the chord changes of the song "How High the Moon." We call this kind of line a *contrafact*. If you were to play "Ornithology" against the melody of "How High the Moon," you'd see that they fit together like lock and key, one active where the other is still and vice versa.

The point is to keep a melody going in your head while playing a counterpoint on your instrument.

Counterpoint on Melody

Level 5. Abstraction

Finally, we come to level 5. This level asks you to make a conceptual leap and imagine the eight bars of "Mary..." as a frame in which you are to improvise. I often ask my students to make a short abstract drawing and then try to play that visual abstraction in the frame of the eight bars of this tune.

Complete Abstraction

These five principles are applicable to any style of music. All you need to do is find the skeletal melody of whatever you're improvising on, and then follow these simple rules. I have worked with people using these ideas on fiddle tunes like "Arkansas Traveler," on jazz standards like "All the Things You Are," and even on movements from the Bach unaccompanied violin sonatas.

The violin performance track on the CD begins with constantly moving quarter notes, and goes through jazz phrasing of a melody. You may practice the remaining levels with the play-along track.

Lamb Chops

Matt Glaser

Skeleton Embedded in Quarter Notes

Skeleton Embedded in Eighth Notes

Jazz Rhythm over Skeleton

Counterpoint on Melody

Complete Abstraction

CHAPTER 2

The Girl I Left Behind Me (Reharmonization)

A beautiful old tune, just as evocative now as when it was first composed, on a date I intend to look up when I get a free minute!

"The Girl I Left Behind Me" is a very familiar melody, but not many people know its name. It's been creeping into my consciousness a lot lately through solos of famous jazz musicians who periodically quote it. I was in a hotel room in Dublin, Ireland, watching an old television clip of Thelonious Monk, who quoted it in one of his solos. When I came back to the United States, I bought a boxed set of my hero, Louis Armstrong, who quotes it in a vocal number entitled, "Rhythm Saved the World."

The focus of our version of this great old Civil War–era tune is to hear a familiar melody played against the backdrop of more interesting and unexpected chord changes—what jazz players call a *reharmonization*. Making up your own "re-harms" is a good way to exercise your ear, although you may incur the wrath of more traditional friends!

As I've stated before, you should always look for the most important core tones in any melody. Interestingly enough, the most important tones in the opening two bars of "The Girl I Left Behind Me" delineate the open strings of the violin in descending order: E on bar 1 beat 1, A on bar 2 beat 1, D on bar 2 beat 4, and G on bar 3 beat 1.

It's very important to keep the core melody tones in your mind. That way, you can simplify your improvisations, which is almost always a better path to take than excessive complexity. Another good practice technique on this tune is to accent whatever notes fall on beats 2 and 4 of the measure. The key to syncopation can be found through accenting the second and fourth quarter notes in a phrase, and even more urgently, the second, fourth, sixth, and eighth notes in a phrase (the "and" of each beat). You won't be playing any complex solos on this tune, but you will be trying to convey a melody with strong and swinging articulation. That's half the battle right there.

You should familiarize yourself with the form of every tune you play, and this one is no exception. Like most fiddle tunes, the overall form is AABB, in which every letter represents eight bars of music.

TRACK 5
"The Girl I Left Behind Me" Full Band

TRACK 6
"The Girl I Left Behind Me" Play Along

The Girl I Left Behind Me

The Infinite Blackberry Blossom (Melodic Cells and Progressive Rhythmic Variation)

Next, we will explore progressive rhythmic variation. We will develop this concept on two tunes. "The Infinite Blackberry Blossom" applies these principles to a descending major scale, while "Ponzi Scheme" applies them to a descending chromatic scale.

Melodies based on descending major scales are ubiquitous. For instance, the much-maligned "Pachelbel's Canon" is essentially a series of melodic variations on a descending major scale bass line. Similarly, the fiddle tune "Blackberry Blossom" could be reduced to a descending major scale as its core melody.

I was never very good at math in school, but the other day I was trying to figure out a math problem related to this tune. If you had twenty distinct variations of a melodic idea, each one four eighth-notes long, how many different ways could you combine these variations on "Blackberry Blossom?" Since there are seven notes in the descending scale, and twenty of these little melodies, I believe the answer would be 7 to the 20th power, which is an incredibly large number that's fifteen digits long. Don't worry, I'm not asking you to play all these variations, nor would it even be possible. My point is simply that starting with very simple phrases in combination, you can quickly generate a vast amount of material for creativity.

There's an old story that illustrates this concept. The court jester and the king were playing chess, and the court jester won. The king said, "I must pay you handsomely for your win." The jester said, "I don't need much. Just put a penny on the first square of the chessboard, then two pennies on the next, then keep doubling the number of pennies on each square as you go." The king said, "Oh, that can't be enough. I need to pay you more." And the jester said, "Don't worry, that'll be fine."

The answer, needless to say, is an extremely high number. The total amount of money on the chessboard is—hold onto your hats— $184,467,440,737,095,516.15.

That jester was crazy like a fox.

If you look at the music for "The Infinite Blackberry Blossom," you will see that in bar 17 we begin using eighth notes, and every four bars, I introduce a new, very simple melodic idea. I call these melodic ideas "cells." You should practice constructing your own melodic cells and playing them on every step of a descending major scale. Experiment by combining these melodic cells and playing different ones on different steps of the scale. At the very end of the music, and at the end of the CD track, you'll hear me begin to play triplets. I'd like you to explore playing triplets on your own, using the same idea of melodic cells. Next, try playing melodic cells in sixteenth notes. We will explore this idea of progressive rhythmic variation further in "Ponzi Scheme."

"The Infinite Blackberry Blossom" Full Band

TRACK 7

"The Infinite Blackberry Blossom" Play Along

TRACK 8

The Infinite Blackberry Blossom

Matt Glaser

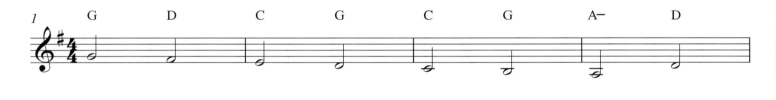

4-Note Melodic Permutations

Here is a partial list of some 4-note groupings that can be used as practice material, in eighth notes, on "The Infinite Blackberry Blossom." The numbers refer to scale degrees. You could play every 4-note unit on each descending scale step, and then begin to combine them. Think of them as shapes to be replicated on each scale degree. If you begin to mix and match them, pretty soon, you'll see why this chapter is entitled "The *Infinite* Blackberry Blossom."

1212	1323	2313
1213	1325	2712
1231	1513	3123
1232	1532	3213
1251	1535	3231
1252	1571	3513
1253	1713	3515
1313	1715	5313
1321	2171	etc.

CHAPTER 4

The Ark and the Saw (Changing the Mode)

The first fiddle tune I learned when I took up the instrument at the age of thirteen was "Arkansas Traveler." I've been playing the fiddle for forty years, and I'm still obsessed with this tune. A beautiful poem by Walt Whitman addresses this state of mind:

> *Beginning my studies the first step pleas'd me so much,*
> *The mere fact consciousness, these forms, the power of motion,*
> *The least insect or animal, the senses, eyesight, love,*
> *The first step I say awed me and pleas'd me so much,*
> *I have hardly gone and hardly wish'd to go any farther,*
> *But stop and loiter all the time to sing it in ecstatic songs.*

In any case, it's a great tune!

My variation on "Arkansas Traveler," which I call "The Ark and the Saw," throws a number of different compositional techniques into the mix. When you understand these principles, try to apply them to a tune of your choice.

The first thing is to maintain the general shape of the melody, as we have discussed in other chapters.

I then changed the mode—in other words, the scale that I was using. Normally, "Arkansas Traveler" uses the notes in a major scale. Here, I based my variation on a pentatonic scale: D, E, G, A, and C, which is a mode of a C major pentatonic scale. I do use other notes in the variation, but those five notes are at the core of what's going on here.

In addition to changing the mode, I tried to fan out the melody over two octaves. Whenever you're working on a fiddle tune, you should always begin by playing the melody in its original location—its original octave. Then, try to play the entire melody either down or up an octave, as the case may be. Finally, you should make up a variation that combines both octaves. This will necessitate making up new melodic material to link the two octaves together.

Another concept at work, in the second full chorus, is that of using open strings as reference points. You'll notice that the second variation is highly abstract, bearing only the slimmest relationship to the original core melody. It is frequently fleshed out with references to open strings. If you experiment with putting in open strings randomly in the middle of melodies, you'll see that the violin helps you create unexpected interval patterns. This is always very impressive to people who don't play the violin, because in the middle of an otherwise stepwise linear melody, you can throw in a note that's far away because it happens to be one of the open strings. Also notice that the timbre (tone color) of these open-string notes can be quite different than those of fingered notes. As long as you're aware of it, it can be a positive attribute to use as an effect.

Although the violin performance on the CD contains the same B section both times through the tune, I've given you an extra B section variation in the music notation. This variation remains in third position the entire time and develops the idea of open strings as reference points. This variation is similar to what I play on the extended performance, which is CD track 1.

TRACK 9

"The Ark and the Saw" Full Band

TRACK 10

"The Ark and the Saw" Play Along

The Ark and the Saw

Matt Glaser

14

18   Remain in third position throughout

22   1.

26   2.

30

33

36

40

CHAPTER 5

Act Natural
(Mutually Exclusive Triads)

There's a great scene in a documentary about the bluegrass singer Jimmy Martin in which Jimmy is plagued by a heckler in the audience. Jimmy says to this fellow, "If you want to horse around with me, we can go out back. I'll be the horse's head, and you just act natural."

When I heard that line, I knew I had to write a tune called "Act Natural." Anyone who has ever heard me play knows that I have a predilection for quoting the Bill Monroe tune "Wheel Hoss." To combine the horse imagery in the anecdote with the tune "Wheel Hoss" seemed an opportunity too good to pass up. So here is "Act Natural."

The tune "Wheel Hoss" itself is very Mixolydian in character, with its strong emphasis on the flatted 7th degree of the scale. I've taken that basic concept and developed it here. You'll notice that the first part of this tune is based on what are called "mutually exclusive triads." Don't be scared; this just means two alternating chords, one of which shares *none* of the notes in the other chord. This melody begins by alternating notes in the G major triad with notes in the F major triad, which don't have any notes in common. It then follows these chords in their inversions going up the scale.

From a technical standpoint, the challenge of these mutually exclusive triads is that they create difficult string crossings. I recommend that you keep your eyes open and look at your bow when playing this. This will help you avoid accidentally bumping into an adjacent open string.

The bridge of this tune offers much needed contrast from the unrelenting eighth notes of the A section by having a more lyrical, sustained bluegrass melody. Experiment with adding double stops to the melody notes indicated. Try a sixth below each note, or a third above each note.

"Act Natural" Full Band
TRACK 11

 "Act Natural" Play Along
TRACK 12

Act Natural

Matt Glaser

CHAPTER 6

High Windy (Developing Motifs and Upper-Structure Triads)

I wrote "High Windy" in 1990 for a friend of mine, Julia Weatherford. Julia and her family live near Ashville, N.C. on a mountain called "High Windy." I thought this was too good a bluegrass fiddle tune name to pass up. "High Windy," like many other tunes, has a core Mixolydian identity, but is also inundated with chromatic-approach tones and *upper-structure triads*—3-note chords that include one or more chord tensions (beyond the 7th).

You'll see that the structure of the A section is based on a repeating melodic motif, which exists in bars 1, 5, 9, and 13. Each time, the answer to that initial statement climbs higher and higher.

- The first answer is in bar 2 and goes as high as a C natural.
- The next answer is in bar 6 and goes up to D natural.
- The next answer is in bar 10 and goes up to E natural.
- Finally, the climactic phrase of the A section is in bar 14, which goes up to B natural before coming to rest on a G sharp.

The last three notes of bar 14 are E, B, and G♯, which spell an E major triad. In the key of D, an E major triad is considered an upper-structure triad, built using the 9, ♯11, and 13. An upper-structure triad can be major or minor. In this case, it's a major triad, created by using ♯11.

Another way to look at the same melodic material would be as scale degrees. Looking at bar 14 this way, the notes would be 1, 3, 5, ♭7, 9, 13, and ♯11.

Always be conscious of what scale degree you are playing. Also, be aware of what key you're in at the moment, and what scale degree you are playing relative to that key. This awareness will help focus your playing and add clarity to your improvisations.

I had a great teacher many years ago named Adolphe Sandole. One of Adolphe's mottos was, "Play in the key, not in the chord." What this means is that it's less important that you know every single chord change in a tune, but more important that you know the key of the moment.

COARSE STRAINS, FINE STRAINS

The A section of "High Windy" is mostly rooted on the lower two strings of the violin with periodic excursions upwards. The B section (starting at bar 17) is almost completely located on the upper two strings.

This hearkens back to an old concept of fiddle-tune playing: the A sections of tunes were called "coarse strains" and B sections were called "fine strains." The reason for this is that the lower strings of the fiddle were made out of thicker, or coarser material, where the upper strings were made of thinner, or finer material. Hence, variations played on the lower two strings are "coarse" variations, and variations played on the upper two strings are "fine" variations.

The melody of the B section creates variety in a different manner from that of the A section. Here, we have a 2-bar motif that develops on gradually ascending degrees of the scale. The melody of the first two bars is oriented around D. Starting at bar 19, the two bars are oriented around E, and starting at bar 21, those two bars are oriented around F♯. The descending lick, which begins in bar 23, is an adaptation of a famous phrase by the great tenor saxophonist Lester Young, from his solo on the tune "Jive at Five" with the Count Basie Orchestra.

Some of the elements in the transcription can be found in the extended performance of "High Windy," which is CD track 2.

 "High Windy" Full Band

TRACK 13

 "High Windy" Play Along

TRACK 14

High Windy

Matt Glaser

CHAPTER 7

IHOP
(Mixolydian String Crossing)

The title of this tune is an acronym, but it does not stand for International House of Pancakes. It also does not stand for "I have omnipotent power," "I have orange pants," "I'm happy optimistic person," or "I hate over-playing." If you think you know what this acronym stands for, please e-mail me your suggestions at mglaser@berklee.edu. If you are the winner, you will receive an e-mail from Matt Glaser! This tune, however, does "hop" from one string to the next, so like many of the etudes in this book, it's great for practicing string crossings, one of the ongoing challenges in the life of any violin player.

Technically, this tune is in the key of B, but it feels like it's in the key of E, my favorite key—a great key on the violin. "IHOP" makes use of the fact that the middle two open strings of the instrument are D and A, thereby imparting a Mixolydian sound to the melody. In this regard, the tune is similar to "Hot Lick Fiddle Chick" and "Act Natural"— tunes that, although in different keys, all share a Mixolydian modality.

The melody to "IHOP" is almost a Rubik's Cube of interlocking melodic elements. The opening two bars form the core melody, which is then transplanted to the B chord, and then to the F♯ chord. Within that 2-bar phrase are many related melodic components. For example, you could choose to develop your improvisation on the alternation between the notes E and D. Or instead, you could choose to elaborate on the 3-note grouping B, F♯, and E. Or, you could develop the gradually ascending phrase: E, F♯, E, G♯, E. All of these melodic units can be found subsumed within the more complicated eighth-note melody of the first two bars.

The bridge of this tune has more of a victorious Bill Monroe vibe. Notice how a change in the melodic rhythm dramatically alters the feeling of the tune. Instead of constantly running eighth notes as in the A section, the bridge has varied rhythms which are more vocal in character. In addition, the melody is high on the E string, at the top end of third position, which contributes to its exultant quality. Be careful of the double chromatic-approach tones, a land mine that this tune shares with "Hot Lick Fiddle Chick."

"IHOP" Full Band

TRACK 15

 "IHOP" Play Along

TRACK 16

IHOP

Matt Glaser

Hot Lick Fiddle Chick (Shifting Positions While Playing Constantly Flowing Eighth Notes)

I wrote "Hot Lick Fiddle Chick" for a friend of mine, Jen Chapman, who, as an adult, decided to take up the violin and become a professional bluegrass fiddler. I told her that although I thought this was a difficult task, I would do my best to help her realize her dream. She was completely obsessed with bluegrass, and to play bluegrass, you must be comfortable playing in the key of B major. Hence, this tune.

Jen was the "Fiddle Chick," and this tune is filled with hot licks. (By the way, Jen got quite good and was able to play gigs.) "Hot Lick Fiddle Chick" begins clearly in the bluegrass idiom, but by the last eight bars or so, it morphs into a twisted bebop tune.

One of the technical challenges of "Hot Lick Fiddle Chick" is shifting between first and third position in the middle of a line. Begin the tune in third position, and use the open A string towards the end of the second bar as a pivot to bring you back to first position. Remain there for close to two bars, and then use the open E string towards the end of the fourth bar as a pivot to shift back to third position. Learn to be comfortable shifting between positions in the middle of a line, and apply this principle to tunes that you already play. You can make up variations that extend from third to first position, and connect the two positions by means of an open string in the middle of the line.

The bridge of the tune, which begins in bar 17, introduces more chromaticism, including single and double chromatic-approach tones. This means that you approach a target note from either one or two half steps away. For instance, the phrase in bar 21 is an example of single chromatic approaches into chord tones. The two pickup notes prior to bar 19 are an example of double chromatic-approach tones, as is the phrase in bar 27. The last four bars of the tune are heavily chromatic, using a lot of standard bebop language, including $\sharp9$ and $\flat9$ degrees of the scale.

TRACK 17 "Hot Lick Fiddle Chick" Full Band

 TRACK 18 "Hot Lick Fiddle Chick" Play Along

Hot Lick Fiddle Chick

Matt Glaser

CHAPTER 9

Gunshot Wound in the E.R. (Dominant Seventh Chords around the Cycle)

A dear friend of mine, Dr. Kalev Freeman, is a fine fiddler and an emergency room physician. Kalev would often come over to my house to play tunes right after he got off his shift in one of Boston's busy emergency rooms. He would always gleefully regale me with horrifying tales of the day's festivities in the E.R. One day, he told me a story about a man whose girlfriend was angry with him and shot him in the chest. The man survived, miraculously, and is no worse for wear. I thought that story deserved a tune, and hence we have my "emergency eighth-note etude," "Gunshot Wound in the E.R."

The main concept behind this tune is the rapid arpeggiation of modified dominant-seventh chords in first inversion, going around the cycle of fifths. You should, of course, have committed to memory the notes in the cycle of fifths.

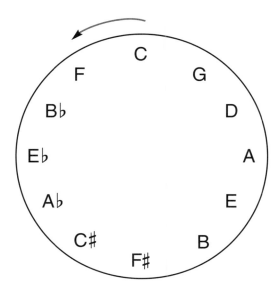

Root movement up a fourth or down a fifth is at the core of harmonic motion in Western music. If you can master this most basic of all chord changes, you will have grasped the simple but indispensable message that jazz has bequeathed to bluegrass.

TRACK 19   "Gunshot Wound in the E.R." Full Band

TRACK 20   "Gunshot Wound in the E.R." Play Along

Gunshot Wound in the E.R.

Matt Glaser

CHAPTER 10

Fishy Hornpipe (Tetrachords)

Continuing with our tradition of smart-alecky harmonic slight of hand (to make tunes more interesting), we have "Fishy Hornpipe." The traditional fiddle tune "Fisher's Hornpipe" is usually played in the key of D major, but sometimes it's played in the key of F major. Each key has its own particular sound, as well as its own particular benefits and drawbacks.

Because I apparently have too much time on my hands, it occurred to me that one could play the tune in the keys of D and F simultaneously. Or, if not simultaneously, then sequentially. So what we have in "Fishy Hornpipe" are four bars in the key of D, then the next four bars in the key of F, and so on and so forth like that.

This approach creates an interesting sound (that of frequent modulation), as well as technical challenges, since you need to reframe your left hand every four bars. One example of this is the important transition from the F sharp (third of the D chord) to the F natural (tonic of F chord).

I recommend practicing the lower and upper *tetrachords*—the first or last four notes of the scale, respectively, in both keys. The lower tetrachord of D major is D, E, F♯, and G. The upper tetrachord in D major is A, B, C♯, and D.

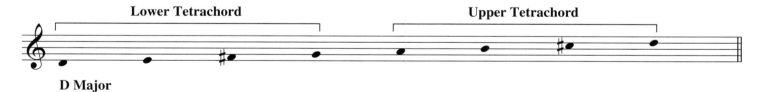

D Major

A tetrachord is named as it is because it is a scale comprised of four notes: a whole step from D to E, a whole step from E to F♯, and a half step from F♯ to G.

The tetrachords in F are as follows: lower is F, G, A, and B♭; upper is C, D, E, and F.

F Major

Get used to practicing tetrachords. They can really orient your hand to the melodic area in which you'll be improvising. The lower tetrachord of D is very different than the lower tetrachord in F. The lower tetrachord of D has an F♯ in it, whereas the lower tetrachord of F has an F natural and a B♭.

Recently, a fine violinist, Sue Buzzard, asked me the question, "How do you practice tetrachords?"

You could start by just rolling them back and forth.

Or you could improvise little melodies that are contained entirely within the four notes.

 "Fishy Hornpipe" Full Band
TRACK 21

 "Fishy Hornpipe" Play Along
TRACK 22

Fishy Hornpipe

Matt Glaser

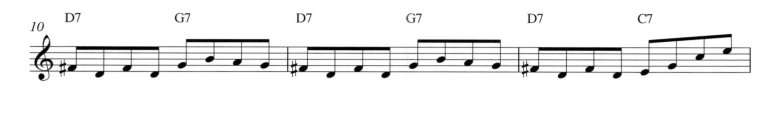

CHAPTER 11

Ponzi Scheme
(Increasing Rhythmic Density)

Ponzi schemes were in the news a lot around the time I wrote this book (spring and summer, 2009). Suffice to say, Ponzi schemes are a class of fraudulent financial dealings in which nobody gets rich except Mr. Ponzi, Mr. Madoff, or whoever is the creator of the scheme. Hopefully, *this* musical "Ponzi Scheme" will artistically enrich everyone who plays it!

In our exercise, "The Infinite Blackberry Blossom," we built large numbers of variations on a descending major scale. In "Ponzi Scheme," we will build a number of variations on a descending chromatic line. The musical inspiration for this exercise came from one of the great organ fugues by J. S. Bach, entitled "The Wedge." (One of my many smart-aleck friends pointed out that a wedge is a pyramid, and a Ponzi scheme is also called a pyramid scheme.) It occurred to me while listening to this Bach fugue that the underlying harmonic structure was similar to that of George Gershwin's song, "Nice Work If You Can Get It." (Of course, running a pyramid/Ponzi scheme, and making lots of money without lifting a finger, would also be "nice work if you can get it!") One could extract a single descending chromatic line that would function as both the melodic skeleton of Bach's fugue, and a guide-tone line for Gershwin's tune.

The exercises in "Ponzi Scheme" begin with constantly moving quarter notes, then move onto constantly moving eighth notes, then eighth-note triplets, and finally sixteenth notes. The tempo and harmonic rhythm remain constant at all times. On the recording, I start with triplets.

I envision what's going on here as a form of tiling. You have a set space and you start by using large tiles, then see if you can pad the whole area with smaller tiles, then smaller tiles yet again. Each time you move up a level of rhythmic complexity, your technical skills on the violin will be challenged.

This is an exercise that you should do on your own to develop your improvisational skills. Take any tune that you play, and try to pad it with constantly moving quarter notes, then all the way through in eighth notes, then eighth-note triplets, and finally sixteenth notes.

The transcription includes sixteenth notes through the A section, but I'm leaving the B section as a puzzle for you to solve. Good luck!

"Ponzi Scheme" Full Band
TRACK 23

 "Ponzi Scheme" Play Along
TRACK 24

Ponzi Scheme

Matt Glaser

CHAPTER 12

That Tumble-Down Shack in Athlone (Guide-Tone Lines in Double Stops)

Here's an arrangement of a beautiful tune that your grandmother might know if your grandmother is hip. It was written in 1918 by Carlo and Sanders. The emphasis in this exercise is to be able to play a melody while simultaneously playing important notes in the guide-tone line. A *guide-tone line* is an alternate melody that brings out important notes in the chord, in a linear fashion. Finding a guide-tone line in a tune is one of the most important things you can do, both to facilitate your own improvisation, as well as to locate juicy notes to play behind a vocalist or another instrumentalist.

Voice leading is the most important part of creating a guide-tone line. Good voice leading implies that your melody should be smooth, linear, and connected, and not jumping randomly. Of course, the epitome of good voice leading is J. S. Bach. Bach had to write an arrangement of a Lutheran hymn for his congregation to sing every Sunday for many years. Bach's approach was to give everybody a good melody to sing, and when you put those four beautiful melodies together, they would create gorgeous harmonic movement.

It is very important that you do not think of chords as static vertical blocks, but instead, as the intersection of beautiful melodies happening simultaneously.

What I have tried to do on this old tune is to play the melody on top and to play nice guide-tone lines in the lower voice. A good way to begin studying this approach is to work on movements from the Bach unaccompanied violin sonatas and partitas. Another way to master harmonically meaningful double stops is to study the studio recordings of the great country fiddler Buddy Spicher. Buddy is a master at harmonizing melodies and exploiting the full double-stop potential of the violin.

TRACK 25   **"That Tumble-Down Shack in Athlone" Full Band**

TRACK 26   **"That Tumble-Down Shack in Athlone" Play Along**

That Tumble-Down Shack in Athlone
Original Tune

Words by Richard W. Pascoe
Music by Monte Carlo and Alma M. Sanders
Copyright 2009 by BERKLEE PRESS

That Tumble-Down Shack in Athlone
Tune with Embellishment

Words by Richard W. Pascoe
Music by Monte Carlo and Alma M. Sanders
Copyright 2009 by BERKLEE PRESS

CONCLUSION

I hope you have enjoyed playing these etudes, and I hope they help you to have fun solving whatever technical and musical challenges come your way. Having a lifelong creative relationship to your instrument is one of the best ways to ensure a healthy, happy life. I know this because I have been lucky enough to be friends with many of the great fiddlers and jazz violinists who have lived and thrived into their ninth decade. In closing I'd like to dedicate this book to some of these fine gentlemen:

> Joe Venuti
> Stephane Grappelli
> Svend Asmussen
> Claude Williams
> Johnny Frigo
> Johnny Gimble

I am not fit to tie their shoelaces, but I am very thankful that I got to know these men in this lifetime.

Thank you, keep fiddling, and don't hesitate to contact me if you have any questions.

—Matt Glaser

About the Author

Matt Glaser is the artistic director of the American Roots music program at Berklee College of Music, and before that, had been chairman of the string department at Berklee for twenty-eight years. Matt is the first and only recipient of the Stephane Grappelli Memorial Award, "In recognition of his significant contribution to the teaching and playing of improvised string music in America," presented by the American String Teachers Association with the National School Orchestra Association. He has performed widely in a variety of idioms ranging from jazz to bluegrass to early music.

Matt has published four books on contemporary violin styles, including *Jazz Violin* co-authored with the late Stephane Grappelli. He has written for many newspapers and music magazines including the *Village Voice*, *Strings*, and *Acoustic Musician*. He has performed with Stephane Grappelli, David Grisman, Lee Konitz, Bob Dylan, J. Geils, Leo Kottke, Joe Lovano, Charlie Haden, Michael Brecker, Kenny Werner, Alison Krauss, Bela Fleck, the Waverly Consort, Fiddle Fever, and most recently with Wayfaring Strangers—a band that fuses jazz and folk music. *The Boston Herald* called him "possibly America's most versatile violinist."

Matt served on the board of advisors of the Ken Burns' *Jazz* documentary, and appears in the film as a talking head. He serves on the board of directors of Chamber Music America and the American String Teachers Association.

Matt has performed at the White House and at Carnegie Hall with Yo-Yo Ma and Mark O'Connor as part of Stephane Grappelli's eightieth birthday concert. He has taught at the Mark O'Connor Fiddle Camp, University of Miami, American String Teacher Association conferences, International Association of Jazz Educator conferences, and many others.

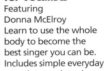